The Delaware Colony

KEVIN CUNNINGHAM

Children's Press®
An Imprint of Scholastic Inc.
New York Toronto London Auckland Sydney
Mexico City New Delhi Hong Kong
Danbury, Connecticut

Content Consultant
Jeffrey Kaja, PhD
Assistant Professor of History
California State University, Northridge

Library of Congress Cataloging-in-Publication Data

Cunningham, Kevin, 1966–
  The Delaware colony / Kevin Cunningham.
      p. cm.—(A true book)
  Includes bibliographical references and index.
  ISBN-13: 978-0-531-25388-5 (lib. bdg.)   ISBN-13: 978-0-531-26601-4 (pbk.)
  ISBN-10: 0-531-25388-5 (lib. bdg.)   ISBN-10: 0-531-26601-4 (pbk.)
  1. Delaware—History—Colonial period, ca. 1600–1775—Juvenile
literature. 2. Delaware—History—1775–1865—Juvenile literature. I. Title. II. Series.
  F167.C86 2011
  975.1'02—dc22   2011007147

All rights reserved. Published in 2012 by Children's Press, an imprint of Scholastic Inc.
Printed in China 62
SCHOLASTIC, CHILDREN'S PRESS, A TRUE BOOK, and associated logos are trademarks and/or registered trademarks of Scholastic Inc.
1 2 3 4 5 6 7 8 9 10 R 21 20 19 18 17 16 15 14 13 12

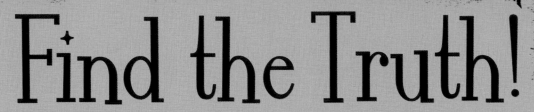

Find the Truth!

Everything you are about to read is true *except* for one of the sentences on this page.

Which one is **TRUE**?

T or F   Delaware once shared a governor with Pennsylvania.

T or F   The French were the first Europeans to settle in Delaware.

Find the answers in this book.

Contents

Washington crossing the Delaware River

4

One of Delaware's Founding Fathers, Thomas McKean

THE **BIG** TRUTH!

Delaware's Founding Fathers

How did these men serve after signing the Declaration of Independence? **36**

After the tea tax, tea sales fell from 900,000 pounds in 1769 to 237,000 pounds in 1772.

TO THE

DELAWARE PILOTS.

THE Regard we have for your Characters, and our Desire to promote your future Peace and Safety, are the Occasion of this Third Address to you.

In our second Letter we acquainted you, that the Tea Ship was a Three Decker. We are now informed by good Authority, she is not a Three Decker, but an old black Ship, without a Head, or any Ornaments.

THE Captain is a short, fat Fellow, and a little obstinate withal.—So much the worse for him.—For, so sure as he rides rusty, We shall heave him Keel out, Overhauling.—and as it is said, he has a good deal of Quick Work about him, We will take particular Care that such Part of him undergoes a thorough Rummaging.

WE have a full worse Account of his Owner:—for it is said, the Ship POLLY was bought by him on Purpose, to make a Penny of us; and that he and Captain Ayres were well advised, of the Risque they would run, in thus daring to insult and abuse us.

Captain Ayres was here in the Time of the Stamp Act, and ought to have known our People better, than to have expected we would be so mean as to suffer his rotten TEA to be funnel'd down our Throats, with the Parliament's Duty mixed with it.

WE know him well, and have calculated to a Gill and a Feather, how much it will require to fit him for an American Exhibition. And we hope not one of your Body will behave so ill, as to oblige us to clap him in the Cart along Side of the Captain.

WE must repeat, that the SHIP POLLY is an old black Ship, of about Two Hundred and Fifty Tons burthen, without a Head, and without Ornaments—and, that CAPTAIN AYRES is a thick chunky Fellow.————As such, TAKE CARE to AVOID THEM.

YOUR OLD FRIENDS,

THE COMMITTEE FOR TARRING AND FEATHERING.

Philadelphia, December 7, 1773.

Monday Morning December 27, 1773.

THE TEA SHIP being arrived, every Inhabitant, who wishes to preserve the Liberty of America, is desired to meet at the STATE HOUSE, This Morning, precisely at TEN o'Clock, to advise what is best to be done on this alarming Crisis.

Timeline of Delaware Colony History

10,000 BCE

The Lenni-Lenape settle present-day Delaware and surrounding regions.

1609

Explorer Henry Hudson reaches Delaware Bay.

1681

Englishman William Penn takes control of the Lower Counties.

1765

The Stamp Act infuriates colonists.

1787

Delaware becomes the first state.

DECEMBER 7, 1787

CHAPTER 1

Original People

The Lenni-Lenape lived in today's Delaware long before European setlers arrived. They also lived in New Jersey and parts of Pennsylvania. These Native Americans organized into **clans** rather than into a large tribe or nation. All of the clans spoke related languages. Some historians believe up to 20,000 Lenni-Lenape may have lived in the Delaware River valley. That was a large population for a Native American group. The Lenni-Lenape were skilled farmers and hunters.

Agriculture was the Lenni-Lenape's main source of food.

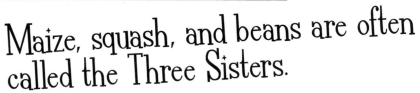

Maize, squash, and beans are often called the Three Sisters.

Crops such as maize (corn), squash, beans, and sweet potatoes could be stored. This guaranteed a food supply for autumn and winter. Lenni-Lenape women tended the farms. They planted the seeds and harvested the crops. Girls helped their mothers and female relatives with farming and cooking. Women also maintained the wigwam. Wigwams were dome-shaped house. They were made of bark placed over a wooden frame.

Most wigwams were 15 to 20 feet (4.5 to 6 meters) wide.

Men hunted and fished. They taught the boys to do the same. Lenni-Lenape often built their wigwams along rivers or shorelines to take advantage of foods found there. They fished from canoes and from the shore. They used nets, hooks, and wooden traps. They also speared fish with harpoons made of deer antlers. Hunters sought birds such as geese and turkeys. Their bows were made from tree branches. The arrowheads were shaped from flint and quartz.

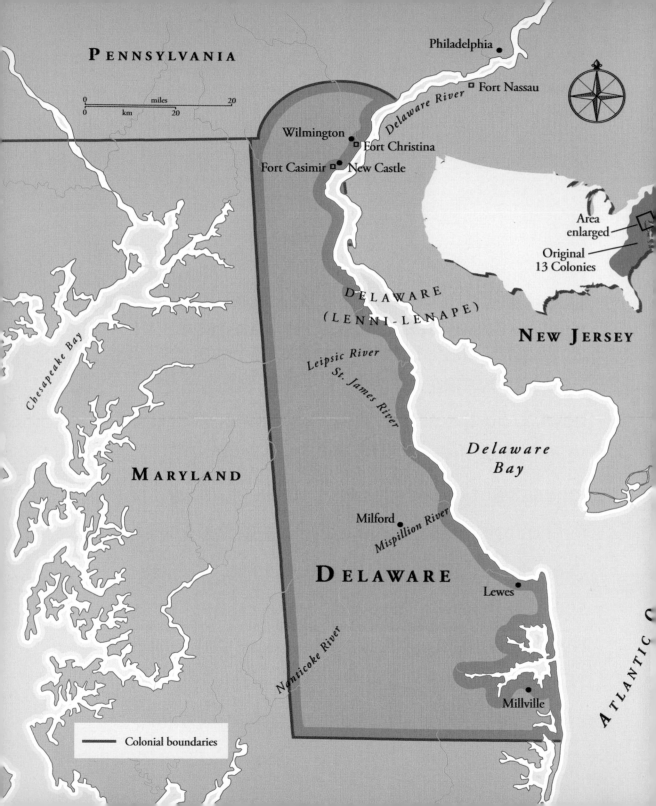

PENNSYLVANIA

miles
0   20
0   20
km

Philadelphia

Fort Nassau

Wilmington

Fort Christina

Fort Casimir   New Castle

DELAWARE
(LENNI-LENAPE)

Area
enlarged

Original
13 Colonies

NEW JERSEY

Leipsic River

St. James River

Chesapeake Bay

Delaware
Bay

MARYLAND

Milford

Mispillion River

DELAWARE

Lewes

Nanticoke River

ATLANTIC O

Millville

Colonial boundaries

CHAPTER 2

Explorers and Settlers

The Lenni-Lenape still inhabited the Delaware region when European ships sailed along the coast in 1524. Explorer Henry Hudson's ship *Half Moon* reached present-day Delaware Bay in 1609. Hudson then sailed north to what is now New York Harbor and the Hudson River. Hudson told his Dutch employers about America's fertile farmland and fur-bearing animals. The Dutch decided to establish trade in the Americas.

The European settlers' farms benefited from the region's fertile soil.

The Pelt Trade

The Dutch West India Company was created in 1621 to control all the Dutch trade in the new **colony**. The company named the lands Henry Hudson had claimed New Netherlands. The Dutch colonists built their first trading post by the Delaware River in 1626. They called it Fort Nassau. They traded with the Native Americans for beaver pelts (skins). These skins were used for warm clothing and hats. They brought high prices in Europe.

Zwaanendael Colony

Dutch settlers set up a second colony near the Delaware Bay in 1631. They named it Zwaandendael (ZWAHN-ehn-dayl). They brought Dutch goods such as iron pots and sturdy duffel cloth to continue their trading with Lenni-Lape. The next year, a Native American chief stole a tin medallion from Zwaanendael to make a tobacco pipe. The colonists complained. The Lenni-Lenape executed the chief because they did not want the settlers to stop trading. This made friends of the chief angry. They burned down the settlement and killed all the colonists.

Zwaanendael means "valley of the swans."

The Dutch traded for furs with the Lenni-Lenape and other native peoples.

New Sweden

The next colony was built by the Swedes in 1638. They called it New Sweden. Part of the colony was a settlement named Fort Christina. It was on the Delaware River. The company that owned New Sweden also wanted to profit from animal pelts. New Sweden

Governor Printz was known for maintaining peaceful relations with the Native Americans and nearby British settlers.

traded with native peoples for 2,200 beaver, otter, and bear pelts in its first year. Johan Printz became governor three years later. Printz introduced tobacco farming to the colony. He also maintained the fur trade.

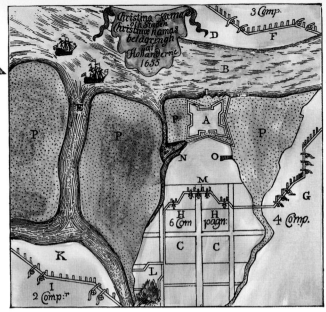

Fort Christina
was named after
Queen Christina
of Sweden.

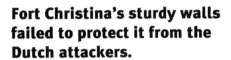

**Fort Christina's sturdy walls
failed to protect it from the
Dutch attackers.**

War Between the Dutch and the Swedes

Printz's final years saw trouble with the nearby
Dutch. In 1655, New Netherland governor Peter
Stuyvesant led 400 soldiers and retook a fort
the Swedes had conquered the previous year.
The Dutch then marched south and attacked
New Sweden's Fort Christina. They destroyed the
Swedish farms. The Swedes at the fort gave up
after two weeks. New Sweden now belonged to
New Netherland. Stuyvesant returned home a hero.

England Takes Control

Stuyvesant's triumph lasted less than 10 years. England captured the settlements of what would become the Delaware Colony in the 1660s. A peace treaty in 1673 gave them the area permanently. William Penn was the governor of Pennsylvania Colony. In 1681, England gave him the area along the Delaware River as well, so his colony would have a route to the ocean. Penn named the settled region the Lower Counties.

In 1696, William Penn wrote about a plan to unite the American colonies.

William Penn founded the Pennsylvania Colony in 1681.

William Penn encouraged a friendly relationship with the Lenni-Lenape.

The Lower Counties

The Lower Counties came into conflict with Pennsylvania's **Quaker** government as they grew. Quakers deeply believed in peace. Pennsylvania's Quaker leaders disapproved of spending money on forts or weapons. France and Spain went to war with England in 1689. French **privateers** were soon raiding settlements. The Quakers still refused to pay for defense. The Lower Counties disobeyed Quaker wishes by forming a **militia**.

Privateer Attack

A ship carrying French privateers raided the town of Lewes in August 1698. The attack lasted for two days. The privateers took everything of value. They also kidnapped the town carpenter and forced him to make repairs to their ship. It was not the first raid. Others had occurred throughout the 1690s. British privateer Captain William Kidd prowled the coast until his capture in 1699. But it once again raised the issue of defense.

French privateer Jean Barth

After creating their own legislature, the people of Delaware still shared a governor with Pennsylvania.

Penn, hoping to keep the peace, allowed the people of Delaware to elect their own legislature.

The situation worsened when Pennsylvania's **legislature** considered sending help to defend New York against the French. The Lower Counties asked why New York deserved help and they did not. Penn was unable to calm the Lower Counties. He allowed them to elect their own legislature to pass laws. This decision was an important step toward Delaware becoming an independent colony.

Colonial Delaware farmers began work before dawn and worked until the sun set.

CHAPTER 3

Life in the Colony

Most settlers in the Lower Counties grew corn and wheat. A smaller number planted tobacco. The workday began before sunrise. Children spent part of the day doing chores such as milking cows or hauling spring water to the house. Farmers used wooden plows edged with iron to till the soil. Wheat was harvested by hand with bladed tools. Colonists held cornhusking parties in late autumn to shuck corn for the winter.

A red ear of corn was a symbol of good luck.

Women at Work

Women raised children and kept house. They also made the family's clothes and prepared meals. Wives and daughters of sheep farmers spun the fleece into wool. Some families grew flax. They spun its fiber into linen. Extra yarn or cloth was sold in nearby towns. Farm meals might include ham or salted pork from slaughtered hogs. Bread was made of wheat or corn. A fireplace provided the cooking fire.

Fireplaces provided farm families light at night and warmth in the winter.

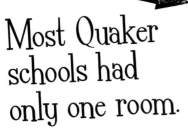

Most Quaker schools had only one room.

Quaker children were encouraged to learn reading and writing to help them study the Bible.

The Colony Grows

New settlers were streaming into the Lower Counties by the early 1700s. Quakers set up many farms. They wore simple clothes and worked hard. They also filled their homes with very plain furniture. They valued education. Children studied reading and writing. Quakers also strongly believed in community service. Children and adults all spent part of their time helping others.

Slaves were bought and sold at auctions.

Scotch-Irish immigrants fled poor conditions and prejudice in England for a life in the colonies. Many came as **indentured servants**. An indentured servant worked several years in return for an employer paying his or her way across the Atlantic. Some farmers and tradesmen purchased slaves. These slaves had been kidnapped in Africa. They worked in fields or workshops. About 1,500 enslaved people lived in the Lower Counties in 1750.

Settlements such as New Castle had grown into bustling towns.

The town of New Castle was Delaware's capital until 1777.

The Lower Counties' population had grown to 35,000 by 1760. This was up from just 3,000 in 1700. But war was brewing on the western **frontier**. Britain had been battling with France and its Native American allies for control of North America. The French and Indian War began in 1754. This war would lead to decisions that split the British from their American cousins for good.

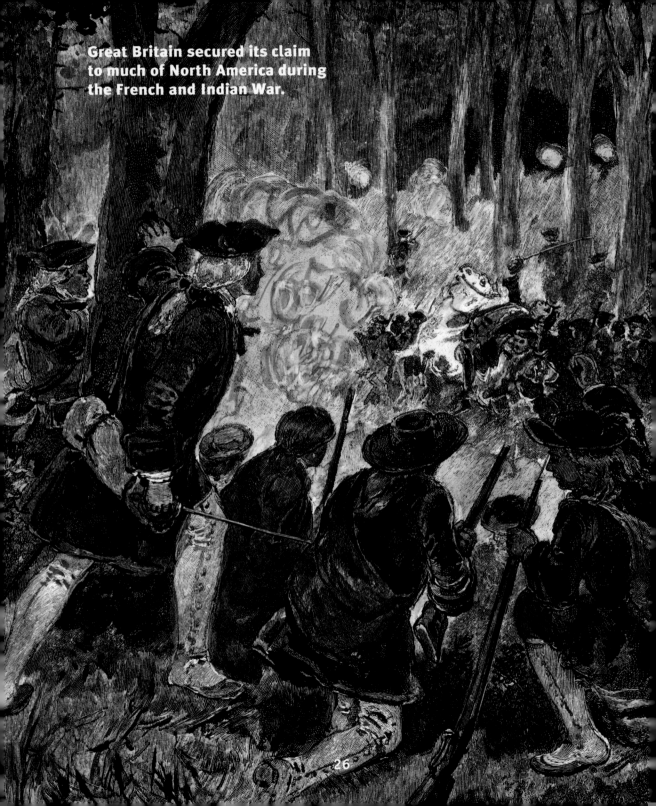

Great Britain secured its claim to much of North America during the French and Indian War.

CHAPTER 4

The Road to Revolution

British forces conquered Montreal after six years of battles. Montreal was a major city in the French colony of Quebec. Great Britain was victorious. But it had gone into debt to pay for the war. Britain also guarded the frontier against hostile American Indians with a number of expensive forts. The British government was in need of money. It began creating new taxes for the colonies.

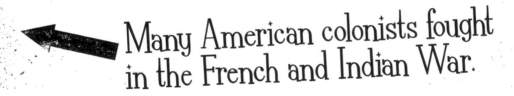

Many American colonists fought in the French and Indian War.

Taxation Without Representation

The first tax was the 1764 Sugar Act. It brought rumblings of unhappiness. The 1765 Stamp Act caused hot anger. Printed material such as newspapers and playing cards needed stamps purchased from the British government. The colonies argued against the act. They were not against paying taxes. They simply believed that Britain had no right to force laws upon the colonies. The colonies had no representatives in Parliament, the British legislature.

Stamps were a common form of taxation in Great Britain.

Many colonists were enraged by the Stamp Act.

The Lower Counties soon joined the rest of the colonies in a **boycott** of British goods. Parliament dropped the Stamp Act because it was worried about the boycott's effect on British businesses. But it passed new taxes in 1766 on goods such as paper and tea. The 1773

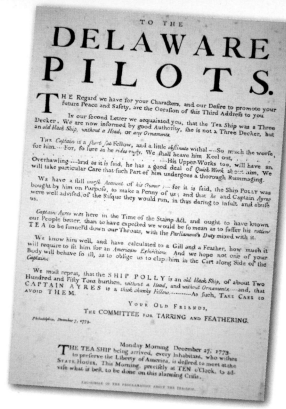

Patriots in Philadelphia warned Delaware against accepting tea from British ships.

Tea Act expanded the rights of the failing East India Company to sell tea in the colonies directly. The price of the company's tea was lowered. This made it cheaper than tea from other companies. Colonists felt this was unfair. They thought it favored British tea too greatly.

Colonists dumped 342 chests of tea into Boston Harbor.

The Boston Tea Party Patriots dressed as Indians to disguise their identities.

The Party in Boston

Patriots opposed to British rule dumped the company's tea into Boston Harbor in 1773. This became known as the Boston Tea Party. Each colony sent representatives to a meeting known as the First Continental Congress the following year. They discussed issues regarding the colonies. One important decision was how to deal with the British. Caesar Rodney, Thomas McKean, and George Read represented the Lower Counties. The Congress sent letters to Britain's government describing the unfairness of the taxes and asking for better treatment.

The Battles of Lexington and Concord began the American Revolution.

The Congress agreed to meet in the spring to discuss the next steps. But the situation changed dramatically on April 19, 1775. British troops clashed with Massachusetts militia groups at small battles in Lexington and Concord, west of Boston. War with Britain looked certain. The Lower Counties began to gather together militia units under a Council of Safety. Rodney, Read, and McKean attended a Second Continental Congress.

Peace Rejected

The Congress sent another letter to Britain. It offered a peaceful end to the conflict. King George III rejected it. Some residents of the Lower Counties didn't wait for the Council of Safety. They traveled south on their own to join Virginians already fighting

George III was the king of Great Britain during the American Revolution.

British troops. Others took part in an unsuccessful invasion of Canada. The Revolutionary War had begun. Now the colonies had to decide whether or not to make a final break from Great Britain.

The Continental Congress included such men as Benjamin Franklin, Thomas Jefferson, and John Hancock.

The Continental Congress thoughtfully debated the issue of independence.

The Second Continental Congress debated throughout June 1776. On July 1, each colony voted on whether to declare independence. Nine colonies said yes. McKean wanted independence. Read was against it. Rodney was back in Delaware serving with the militia. There was a tie without his vote. Each colony got only one vote. The Lower Counties' vote was considered to be undecided. The Congress agreed to take a second vote the next day. They hoped that all 13 colonies would give **unanimous** support to independence.

Rodney's Ride

Rodney received word of the tie from McKean the night before the second vote. Rodney set out on an 80-mile (129 km) ride on horseback and by carriage through a crashing thunderstorm. He arrived at Independence Hall in Philadelphia the next day. His boots and spurs were covered in mud. He voted with his friend McKean for independence. Read changed his vote to yes so that the Delaware delegation was unanimous. All three men signed the Declaration of Independence.

Rodney's ride was later included on the back of Delaware's state quarter.

Delaware's soldiers fought at the Battle of Long Island in August 1776.

Blue Coats

The Lower Counties were now called Delaware. They began to put together a state government. Meanwhile General George Washington and the Continental army faced British redcoats at the Battle of Long Island. Delaware soldiers in blue coats and buckskin pants fought there and at White Plains, New York. The Americans lost both battles. These defeats sent the Continental army across the Delaware River into Pennsylvania. The colonies faced disaster. But the war had barely begun.

Delaware's Founding Fathers

Delaware's signers of the Declaration of Independence faced an unusual situation. Each colony had one vote for or against a break with Great Britain. But Delaware's representatives were split. Thomas McKean wanted independence. George Read opposed the Stamp Act and other British taxes. But he voted against the Declaration. Caesar Rodney had to cast the tiebreaking vote for independence during a second vote on July 2. Delaware took up the fight against Britain from that day.

George Read

Read at first believed that the colonies should try to solve their problems with Britain rather than declare independence. He served as a U.S. senator and chief justice of the Delaware Supreme Court after the war.

Thomas McKean

McKean was a lawyer of Scotch-Irish background. He supported independence early on. McKean was president of the Continental Congress when the Revolutionary War ended. He later served as Pennsylvania's governor and chief justice of the Pennsylvania Supreme Court.

Caesar Rodney

Rodney was honored on the Delaware U.S. quarter that was released in 1999 because of his famous ride to cast Delaware's deciding vote for independence. He was a general in the Delaware militia during the war. He spent much of his time battling pro-British Loyalists and privateers in the Lower Counties.

The battles that followed Washington's crossing of the Delaware are often considered a major turning point in the war.

The Delaware River was full of ice as Washington and his men crossed it on Christmas Day 1776.

The Battle of Trenton

Washington counted on a daring attack to rally his troops. Twenty-four hundred men crossed the Delaware River through a snowstorm on Christmas night. The Continental army's attack on Trenton, New Jersey, the next morning surprised a camp of German soldiers hired by Britain. The short battle ended in a Continental army victory. The British were stunned. But British troops entered Delaware the following spring. They captured Wilmington, one of the colony's major towns.

John Haslet

John Haslet was born in Ireland. He was a minister, soldier, and physician before taking command of the First Delaware Regiment in the Continental army. The Delaware Regiment was among the last to retreat at White Plains. Haslet fell into the water during the famous crossing of the Delaware River into Pennsylvania with Washington. But he participated at the Battle of Trenton. He was killed just a week later at the Battle of Princeton.

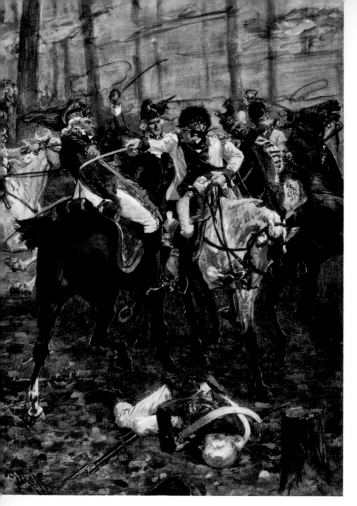

Many Delaware men fought in the bloody Battle of Cowpens.

Blue Hen's Chickens

Delaware troops were considered among the best in the Continental army. Their bravery earned them the nickname Blue Hen's Chickens. This name came from a breed of fighting roosters. Sixty Blues stood in the fighting line at Cowpens (South Carolina) in January 1781. It was one of the most important battles of the war. Only 10 Blues survived. But the British were defeated.

Delegates voiced their concerns and debated details about a constitution at the Constitutional Convention.

There were 55 delegates to the Constitutional Convention.

The war ended in October when the British surrendered to Washington at Yorktown. It soon became clear that the new nation needed a **constitution** to bind together the former colonies. A constitutional convention met at Philadelphia in 1787. These men wrote what became the U.S. Constitution. The Delaware representatives worried that the new document would allow large states to overpower small ones.

The First State

A plan called the Great Compromise called for two houses of Congress. One house called the Senate allowed each state the same number of representatives no matter how large or small the state. The other was called the House of Representatives. Its seats were based on population. The new constitution went to each state for approval. Delaware approved the document on December 7, 1787. It was the first state to do so. The First State became Delaware's official nickname in 2002. ★

DECEMBER 7, 1787

The Delaware state flag was adopted on July 24, 1913.

True Statistics

Number of Lenni-Lenape before Europeans arrived: 20,000

Year Zwaanendael was founded: 1631

Number of slaves in the Lower Counties in 1750: About 1,500

Population of the Lower Counties in 1700: 3,000

Population of the Lower Counties in 1760: 35,000

Length of term for an indentured servant: 5 to 7 years

Number of signers of the Declaration of Independence from Delaware: 3

Number of Continental army soldiers at the Battle of Trenton: 2,400

Number of states that approved the U.S. Constitution before Delaware: 0

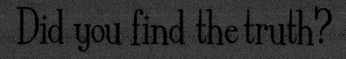

Did you find the truth?

 T Delaware once shared a governor with Pennsylvania.

 F The French were the first Europeans to settle in Delaware.

Resources

Books

Blashfield, Jean F. *The Delaware Colony.* Mankato, MN: Child's World, 2004.

Cheripko, Jan. *Caesar Rodney's Ride.* Honesdale, PA: Boyds Mill, 2004.

Downey, Tika. *Delaware.* New York: PowerKids Press, 2010.

Dubois, Muriel L. *The Delaware Colony.* Mankato, MN: Capstone, 2006.

Hazen, Walter A. *Everyday Life: Colonial Times.* Culver City, CA: Good Year, 2008.

Marsh, Carole. *Delaware Native Americans.* Peachtree City, GA: Gallopade International, 2004.

Miller, Amy. *Delaware.* New York: Children's Press, 2009.

Welsbacher, Anne. *Delaware.* Mankato, MN: Capstone, 2003.

Organizations and Web Sites

The Delaware Nation
www.delawarenation.com
Study the history of Delaware's Native American peoples and learn what is happening in the Delaware/Lenni-Lenape Nation today.

Delaware Public Archives
http://archives.delaware.gov
Find documents, photos, and other resources connected to Delaware's past.

Places to Visit

Delaware History Museum
504 Market Street
Wilmington, DE 19801
(302) 656-0637
www.hsd.org/dhm.htm
See a Revolutionary War flag, George Washington's chair, and other pieces of Delaware history at this museum run by the Delaware Historical Society.

Fort Christina State Park
East Seventh Street
Wilmington, DE 19801
(302) 652-5629
www.nps.gov/history
/history/online_books
/explorers/sitec12.htm
Visit the site of New Sweden's first settlement.

Important Words

boycott (BOI-kaht)—a refusal to buy goods from a person, group, or country

clans (KLANZ)—social groups that are smaller than a tribe and larger than a family

colony (KAH-luh-nee)—an area settled by people from another country and controlled by that country

constitution (KAHN-sti-TOO-shun)—the laws of a country that state the rights of the people and the powers of government

frontier (fruhn-TEER)—the far edge of a settled territory or country

indentured servants (in-DEHN-shurd)—people who agreed to work a certain amount of time in return for paid transportation to the colonies

legislature (LEJ-is-lay-chur)—a group of people who have the power to make or change laws

militia (muh-LISH-uh)—a group of people who are trained to fight but who aren't professional soldiers

privateers (prye-ve-TEERZ)—armed men given permission by a government to raid enemy ships and territory

Quaker (KWAY-kur)—a member of the Society of Friends, a religious group that believes in equality and nonviolence

unanimous (yoo-NAN-uh-muhs)—agreed upon by everyone

Index

Page numbers in **bold** indicate illustrations

About the Author

Kevin Cunningham has written more than 40 books on disasters, the history of disease, Native Americans, and other topics. Cunningham lives near Chicago with his wife and young daughter.